Odo Simon Agbo studied at the University of Roehampton, London, and Nnamdi Azikiwe University, Awka, in Nigeria, where he obtained a Master's Degree in Project Management and a B. Tech. degree in Biotechnology, respectively. He rather sees writing as part of life. Currently, he lives in Doha, Qatar. He is the Senior HSEQ Consultant & Business Development Executive for Bravo Qatar. He previously worked as a Corporate QHSE Manager with Advanced Offshore & Marine Solutions at Qatar Shipyard Technology Solutions. He is the author of several unpublished books. The Dancing Sun is his second book.

Dedicated to a new African renaissance, innovative and purposeful leadership in Nigeria, global peace and harmonious co-existence among different cultures and ethnicities in Africa and in every nation of the world.

Odo Simon Agbo

THE DANCING SUN

A Collection of Poems

AUSTIN MACAULEY PUBLISHERS™

LONDON • CAMBRIDGE • NEW YORK • SHARJAH

ISBN – 9789948762652 – (Paperback)
ISBN – 9789948762645 – (E-Book)

Application Number: MC-10-01-0317512
Age Classification: 17+

Printer Name: iPrint Global Ltd
Printer Address: Witchford, England

First Published 2024
AUSTIN MACAULEY PUBLISHERS FZE
Sharjah Publishing City
P.O Box [519201]
Sharjah, UAE
www.austinmacauley.ae
+971 655 95 202

My special thanks and appreciation go to the Editorial Board of Austin Macauley Publishers for recognizing that I have a voice that deserves to be heard. They told me what I did not know about this book in their editorial comments informing me of their decision to publish the work: "We can confidently state that your work was found to be a very interesting read. Each book of "Affairs of the Heart," "Affairs of Men," and "Issues of Life" has been written in creative and easy-read poetic language. You succeeded in catching the reader's attention and interesting[sic] to the topic of this poetry. You have opened a new horizon to whom looking forward to the illumination of the soul in life." I can say that those lines are the strongest motivation I have ever received to keep writing.

I thank the production team for their tireless, meticulous artistry in typesetting and formatting the interior and for the cover design of the book.

Table Of Contents

Prologue

Merchants Of War

This is unfortunate, Africa!
How unfortunate you are, Africa; unfortunate and unlucky,
Africa.
Unlucky and unfortunate, Nigeria.
Unfortunate and unlucky, Algeria.
Unlucky and unfortunate, Liberia.
Unfortunate and unlucky, Libya.
Unlucky and unfortunate, Egypt.
Who did this to you?

What's caused you this great evil?
Nature's so generous, man's so wicked.
The crusts of thy earth are so rich,
Richly endowed with black gold,
With gold, silver, and precious metals.

Thy ambiance is endowed with beauty –
Pleasant seasons and clement climates.
The soils of thy earth are firm and compact.
Not easily given to quakes and shakes.
Nor do raging sounds of volcanoes,
And eruptions menace your lands,

For your maker has spared you from being in the line of fire,
Of the Traumas from misfortunes of Tornadoes, Katrinas, and wildfires.

Reserving such for the races and the nations,
Preserving and residing with the state of arts and technologies,
Designed and maintained to contend with the stated cursed ecologies.
For you're not afflicted with frosts and snows as those other nations.

Abundantly provided for by nature,
Abandoned and impoverished by hunger and lack,
Perpetually raged with war and malnutrition
Pitiably ravaged by disease and assorted deprivations.

Your Ports are besieged by merchants of war.
Flooded with heavy military wares and belligerent vessels.
Artilleries, tanks, grenades, and life-threatening ballistic missiles.
Traded by warmongers and alien mercenaries,
Celebrating in your docks, shores, and harbors.
The largest trade fair sites for the exhibition of their might,
Super-sophisticated arms and ammunition
Converged to incite kits against their kins.
In place of volcanic sounds and eruptions,
And raging noise of earthquakes and ocean surge,
Are plaguing sounds of machine guns and armored tanks,
As grenades are ceaselessly generated from your homes for your homes,

Where brothers have been pitched against brothers
As these merchants of wars, with generous arms aid and trade
Incite your sons and daughters to wars and killings,
Sparking off these interplays of bloodletting
In these endless pogroms.

Who hast done this to you, Africa?
Who in haste has gunned you down, Sudan, Mali, Rwanda,
and Somalia?
What about you, Eritrea, and Ethiopia?
In your perplexion, I probed my own perplexity.
Peradventure, our complexion is the problem.
Are we created inferior in mind and knowledge?
Or slated for interiors of mines of ignorance?

Then I traced your agony
And trailed your woes.
To the advent of the fair-skinned
Merchants of treasures and labor
Explorers of leisure and pleasures
Gobblers of wealth of nations
Galant seekers of knowledge and wisdom
Giant sinkers of noble causes by minor nations.

They set aside your science and cultures.
And cast down the altars of your gods.
And set up monuments in memory,
Of their own beliefs,
They carted away your golds and ornaments.
Repatriated your culture of love and communion.
Partitioned your kingdoms into shreds of imbeciles.

And sowed seeds of hatred within these sects of impossibilities.

They destroyed your psyches and stole your minds.
They subjugated your civilization and stowed your mines.
They sapped your adventurous spirits and sowed poverty.
For the worst poverty that can menace any race,
Or even a generation of a people is not the poverty.
Of materials of food.
Nor does hunger of food kill to death.
Rather he is poor whose mind has been made captive.
Captive of false beliefs and conspiracy theories.
And whose soul's been traded for vain.
In exchange for their gains of this world.

Cain and Abel

Make the hay while the sun shines.
Haste to hell while Cain thrives.
Break the yoke while Abel lasts.
Release the neck while the debtor struggles.
Decrease the tricks while the storm rumbles,
Before it's late when the thunder storms.
Forfeit the loots while the manna descends.
For danger looms when the Angels re-ascend.

Retrace your steps while the hammer hangs.
Forever stink hence the hammer bangs.
The morn will come when the rest's relaxed.
Strive to laugh while the best lasts.
The dawn of doom's when the heart bleeds.
Bleed to death, the lone price that breeds,
For the heart that hates – a heart that bleeds.
A heart that bleeds is the heart of Cain; that dies.

Book One
Affairs of the Heart

The Heart of Man

The heart of the matter is a matter of the heart.
The affairs of men are ruled and mastered by the heart.
The lasting principles: be open as you may need,
In affairs that link the hearts of men.

A wise Don says in years past,
The affairs of the heart are too deep to retrieve,
From the heart of man,
That holds brief for the might,
There's no how to know the mind of the heart,
From the face of the man that's a mask.

Be masters of the heart, and you'd be master of the world.
For the cunnings of men are treasured in the heart.
With frailty of the mind, we play to a hostage.
The heart of the man, the center of greed –our host.
The craftiness of the heart, the siege that holds,
The Equations of life that are balanced in the heart.
A good heart brings forth a craftily good man.
A bad one breeds a craftily demonic mind.

The Black Vineyard

Dark like a Black, you soiled my thoughts.

Back from the blues, I boiled with lusts.

Pure like gold you bought my gaze.

Few and bold, we fought for your face.

For you to swirl, we scramble like ants.

The rest would be filled to gamble with your pants.

For me, it would be enough if I struggled with your breasts.

Although it would be gain to be settled with a kiss.

Your breasts are like the Apple that unsettled some of the Angels.

Your gaits are like a castle; I fancied they're yours.

That some would withdraw we coil with hate.

For fear I might lose, I toil like "Job"[1].

The battle for your love, a battle I'll win.

They rattle like the bird and prattle that I limp.

---

[1] Reference to the struggles of the Biblical character, Job.

Higher Than Truth

High the stakes and stake the lot.

Lift the odds and risk a loss.

Hide the swords and woo the flock.

Dangle the whip, and there's a brisk flop.

Tumble the facts, and there's a brief bloom.

Rumble a Fast; there's a bleak gloom.

Fetch the False there's a gain in Faith.

Face the truth; there's a drop in gain.

Regain the body; risk the soul.

Reclaim the soul; lose the man,

Rebuild the duo; enthrone the mind.

The mind of man slave of a quest.

The quest for shadows robbed the Real:

The Nature and Man, captive of fear.

Brutal Love

Milano Risky bragged like he's drunk.
From that moment dragged his frame as a cart.
Came to the race with no trace he's drunk.
Settled his manhood in a site he'd explore –
a place of pleasure yet to be exploited by a man,
Some men would think it's a leisure of some sort,
And loosen their mind.
And take the act with a measure as a sport of a kind.

He came and settled in the interiors of her nest as a pest.
And poured the slime that'd hatch the eggs she breeds,
He paid the virgin that's laden with innocence of reason,
And pegged the bargain stiffly like a brute,
And thrust his spear swiftly across her thighs,
Like a Comet across the skies.
He bought her pride with a price of his own, as passion.
And wrought her ruin, a debt of frailty of gender,
Cowed like an ewe, she bled to death with erosion of blood.
Milked in a process, a struggle to live with the shame,
Indiana vented her despair on the gory event that betrayed.
And is flown to a land that she'd never owned.
But is blown into a peace that she'd never known.

Nostalgia

I die to see you soon;
To see my beautiful heart;
To behold your pretty smile;
To sing our song of love.

I die to dine with you again;
To do what we know how to gain;
To sacrifice our feelings for self;
To die for each other's love.

By quenching the thirst of your mind,
I'll kill the hunger of my soul,
As you lie resting in my bosom,
And I reclose upon your breasts.

Women

Someone told me she's brought out of the man.
The same one's bold to say she's wrought to woo men.
Then I thought I could know who's the woman,
And I sought the breadth of my mind to seek the woman.
But like the makeup of all rational beings,
She will defy my knowing till I entered,
The mind of a child to see her as in infant.
For who can ever know the woman, even their own woman

Breakup

Gone are the days when the hearts were young and gay.
While in romantic ways did not roll in the hay.
While laying close,
Solaced in each other's humors and smiles.
Paid deaf heed to folk's probing rumors and spites.

Bloomed and groomed the other,
Stunted and crude in knowledge.
Of life, of ideas, and ideals.
Of charters, principles, and rules.
Scattered in mind and heart.
Full of fears and tears.
Cos tomorrow's so uncertain to breach,
Gripped with the need to be bridged,
In bodies and hearts; in slothful indolence,
As to provide for now and the tomorrows.
Yet a yearning appetite rules
Perpetual appeasement with pleasures.

One nurtured and tutored the other – the unregenerate.
Now indispensable hands of distance tears apart.
Hard realities of the racing pace of time, devastates.
While one struggles to grapple with this shock,
The shock and the challenges.
Of becoming a man.
Called to serve the globe in a world-class sense.
For his part, he's focused in reverent commitment,
To the resolve to live for each other even in storms.
We are each caught up, I suspect,
In the woods and the gloom, I expect.
Poring over,
And numbering, as the case may be,
Storing in,
And mumbling the regrets we reared,
Tumbling thoughts in minds,
Fears threat the bets we had:
Of the moments we shared.
Of the times cherished.
Of the experiences dared.
And the secrets shared.
Of expectations in contrast with realities.
Of promises not kept.
Or rather, demands not met.
Deeds innocently given.
Actions insatiably received.
Bids gallantly won.
Auctions empathically lost.
Of joys gleefully generated
Pains generously borne.
Of hurts painstakingly avoided.

Blames consciously ignored.
Rights glaringly denied.
Privileges openly abused.
Treasures selfishly exploited.
Endowments lavishly used.
Gained vantages cheerfully untapped.
Of the gratifications sacredly delayed.
Of rights and benefits so kindly overlooked.

And how much less-deserving now,
As we expend productive energy.
Grieving over imaginary offenses.
Nursing imported hurts.
You forget so casually?
Someone so costly attached
To you in heart, in will,
He chose to sacrifice so much –
Comforts, pleasures, and others for your sake?
Or completely fight not to recall,
The one,
He made you for a time,
You mean so much to yourself.
Because events have bored
Drastic vents in our vows:
For better for worse.
In sickness and health bla bla….
And our resolve to share one cot,
Under hails and storms,
For a test, as he believes,
Of true natures and trust?
Could one believe he would hear stories,

Of you only from the folks?
How would he content with living,
With the memory you're dead
While you live.

You refuse to release yourself to liberty.
He refrains to reduce the man to servitude.
You'll understand his plight, this dilemma,
And may realize the price of course.

His heart recoils within.
His thoughts becloud at the peak.
Each time to think of it is worse,
Acquiring a new heart for his soul,
Or even a new mate for his bed.
He's made that initial mistake for a stake,
Selling his heart to you at a loss.

Could you just come back the way you're?
He feels and understands your pity plight there.
He seems to discern your pretty fright too:
Things have not turned out either the way you expect,
For this, you lack the face to give.
For that, you fail to note as well,
The blood exchange for one on end.
For that alone and for the others you know.
He endures the grief and gives in
To sorrows for the waste, you've been.
And worries for the way you behave.

You refuse to heed and respect,
That voice of all decorum should rule.
You withstand the urge of reason,
That courtesy at all should prevail.
To listen to his voice any more at times.
From the other end of the wires and lines,
For these and for once he's fed up in truth,
With this success:
Of failing to revert you to type.

Is this justifiable at first,
You bite the fingers that fed you even for a day?
He seems not to know that answer at once.
Look, he's left all to history to judge.

One wishes he could make you happy,
Perhaps he could put smiles on your face.
Would that he could fulfill your wildest dreams.
Satisfy your unguarded desired wishes.
For unlimited spoils without toils.
One wishes you could remember him with relish.
In lieu of regrets and disgusts,
One wishes you could discuss him as you need,
With a bit of charity and with truth.
How come these defaming sarcasms?
With those reported hate and scorns.
One wishes you tell them, the folks,
His true natures which you know.
But those make-belief stories,
Cooked up to woo sympathy,
Could justify this wild–goose chase?

One wishes he gets a bit of roles.
In the constructive re-engineering,
Of the pieces of this life you own,
Shattered.
So broken by no other but you.

One wishes you could send back *Nwanyidugwu*
His daughter by rite of culture.
Your daughter by right of proximity.
For proofs – who remains one's heartbeat till now.
One wishes above all you could come back.
Ogobuchi asks to find out from you:
"Mommy, why did you leave us?"
And daily pesters dad with questions:
"Daddy, where's mommy?"
Please do kindly send us answers.

But how could I forget you O! **Akuchi**?
Why should I not forgive you O! My miss?

Whatever be the case,
Let's conclude the task,
And close the ranks:
Distance is a test.
Time is a pest.
Eating away our dreams and visions,
Crippled by incapacitations and inabilities.
More aptly, lack of access
To basic facilities to draw us close again,
Or impoverished by the failure,
Of the national economy to give us back.

Our time and talent investments there into.

I am tied in wish and will alone.

But will not be tired of waiting and looking along.

To see if I could come to your good books.

Or you show up to betray this loss

My Love!

My love is impeccable from head to toe.

My love is the perfection of everything that is beautiful.

My love is a quintessence of all that is pretty.

Her waist is as slender as spider's.

Her hips are as wide as the center of the Figure 8

Her buttocks are as high as an anthill,

And as level as a descending waterfall.

Her breasts are as light and weightless as the coconut head, rid of water.

Her shoulders are as high in width as the head of Figure 8.

Her abdomen is as flat as an air-less tube.

And as unrumpled as an inflated balloon

Her eyes are as bright as a cat's and as attractive as tsetse fly's.

Her mouth is as round as a semi-circle.

Her heart is as pure as purity in its elements.

My Angel

A messenger appears on earth.
And against all odds unearths.
The young man with the revealing realization,
Of his innate power of bravery,
Can save his nation from slavery.
Gideon raised a monument of pride.
In memory of the momentous encounter:
"The Lord my Peace,"

Gideon looks at the harbinger of the hope.
Gideon calls her an Angel.
An Angel is a harbinger of peace.
Brings out the bests in men.
From a stupor she spurs into profitable endeavors.

Angels since ancients have been.
Sterling example of patient beings.
Never taken to offence at men's excuses,
Nor easily angered that men are vastly prone,
To cling to weaknesses of their nature.
Tactfully persuading, she stems,
The tide of self-imposed weaknesses,
She inspires men to conviction:

Battles are not lost or won.
Until they are fought and won.

An Angel is a messenger of hope.
Generates threshold escape velocity.
And propels beyond gravitational forces:
Of self-limitation, doubts, and unbelief.

I know someone.
This one's brought calm.
Bestowed stability to emotional qualms.

Is it a He or a She? I know not.
I know she or he lived.
And existed as flesh and blood.

You bring peace to this turbulent inner man.
You inspired self-possession for this expired self.
You tutored me: "think highly of yourself".
You featured me in events highly profiled.
Ignored shortcomings, though multiple-numbered.
You opened the door to your heart in trust.
Without terms for fear of hurts.
You fed me with this sense of worth.

You exhumed this image of self –
Hitherto buried in the **uglies** –
In memories of background grooming.
Of childhood memories that's proved gloomy.
A good friend like you is an Angel.
You ran with me and hunted with me.

Always there in body or in spirit –
A seal of our friendship.

In pains, in comfort; joys or sorrows,
In safety, danger; scandal or praise,
In a crown, in shame or robe of glory,
In a garb of success or shackles of failure –
You're always by me thinking and believing,
There could be a positive change.
Wherefore inspiring to be the best.
Of what I am:
You are an Angel!

A priceless friend like you is an Angel.
Who came in handy in my quest,
For the meaning and definition,
Of purposes for life.
In connection with the rest of humankind.
In case I'd give them the best:
You are an Angel!
Angels come to men from God.
Angels act as windbreaks from above,
To the excesses of our nature as men,
In conscience and in truth.

For stubbornness of heart, you scolded.
Weakness of resolve, you plodded.
Ignorance of mind, you tutored.
Frailty of body; the spirit, you propped.
Enervated; exhausted, your presence strengthened.
Meanness of effort,

Meager measure of success,
You still appreciated.
You are an Angel!

In innocence of mistakes,
Your face was brave.
In sincerity,
You forgive all faults.
Knowing someday and somehow
I could become better.
Always inspiring that I be.
The best that I can be.
You are an Angel!

In the light of your firmness,
It's mistaken for nagging.
Yet your incessant admonitions,
Healed this age-long habit.
You taught us:
Hate the deed.
Love the doer.
Beyond equivocation, there're proofs.
You love me for what I am.
Never for what I do or have.
You convinced me it did not matter.
Where or what I was.
Rather, a hunger for change.
Believing I could change somehow, someday.
You are an Angel!
By my sick bed you sat.
When the rest of my friends had spat.

Inducing life into my famished body,
My ailing spirit.
With gentle strokes of tender fingers,
And with intermittent flashes,
Of smiles and unfailing face,
With the aromatic fragrance of your sebum.
You assured you were not without hope yourself.
Making me believe I could not be on the wrong path after all.

You want me to sit up.
You want us to chat one-to-one.
But lo! My nerves are stiffened,
And my bones are clogged up.
While the realization dawned on your understanding,
I'm not in the least blamed,
You stoop low to my ears,
Reminiscing our good old years.
Equipped with a fleet recital.
Of the pleasant, sweet memories,
You prolong my stay.
Albeit deep engulfment with fears of eventualities,
You exude this confidence in fate.
Gleefully executed to procure revival,
For my fading hope of survival.
With tactful squeeze of my palms.
And tickling cuddles of my cheeks.
You inject fresh blood into my veins.

As I journeyed on my heart sank,
As the limitless ocean of distance struck –
And emerge in front of me.

Enmeshed in good deeds undone.
Then my breathing quickened.
But while my tympanic membrane,
Geometrically dimmed and waned.
Like from an ageless stream of miles.
I still heard your screams and sighs.
"Even though it be now,
"Divine master, keep his soul,
In the safety of your safe."

With a final hiss of sigh.
And a parting kiss of resignation.
You release my hand,
Smoothing my homeward path,
With this downpour of tears.

Only then did I somehow understand your fears.
Your humanness has gotten the better part of you.
But what could I do?
Without just wanting to,
I honorably bowed out.
Knowing somehow, someday,
We could see again in the beyond.
For you are an Angel!

A Pool of Death

Busy and choking,
The Lagos traffic clusters.
Fleeting glimpse unmarred,
There's this fleeing ardor of the day.
She's spotted in the conglomerate.
Among commuters, seeking asylum.
The improvised Bus Stop suffices.
Peeping and shying away,
in a mood for a Bus to Stop,
From pelting splashes from dark clouds
Against the sands on ground.
Worsening plights amidst rumors,
Another hike in the price of energy looms.
Petrol stations no longer afford.
To keep those engines running as needed.
Refineries are feared to be running dry.

Mindless mad scramble?
Can this be descriptive enough?
Of this attitudinal approach.
To this national reproach.
Waiting to catch a public means.
To quickly get away from this madness –

But this is preferable:
Landing a plum-executive "lift".
Can be usual of average females –
The habitual weekend traveler.
Women!
Easily prone to wanting all things at no cost.

Then follows the squealing brakes.
The pads of the young car screeching.
United with smoke-emitting display,
From three-week-old tyres,
Of a priced Benz that's the vogue.
Swerving irresponsibly to the sides.
She comes irrepressibly to an unprecedented halt.
Orchestrated by the sight of that frantically waving damsel.
That could turn out to be one of the highly-priced rogues.

It'll be unusual.
Had this not generated,
These over-dose of name-calling –
"Oloshi! Oloriburuku!! O ti ya we-re!!!"
Other road users are yelling.

Was I in the least regretful.
Bothered by these public emissions of curses?
After all situation's fully in control.
And the realization truly attained,
Another weekend's been surely gained.

At last, there's a craning of the neck,
A thrusting forth of the head.
With the torso in likewise manner,
Projected through the side window.

And with the Agama Lizard gesture:
Invitation is nodded across to the lady in question.
With the protruding head of course.
The understanding is successfully consummated.
For she in the long run as expected,
And as elegantly as required,
Has begun to drift towards my "new baby".
Just like oil against a sloping topography.

II
As acquaintanceships are universally certified,
I sought a deeper meaning and gain,
Into our sort of breeding union, my bane.

Thus, I threw my doors ajar.
With an invitation at bay.
For the knowledge at par.
Of a closer affair as a pair.
As I'm wont to do in the past.
After all it's another weekend in the month.
And justifiably for that matter.
I need a fresh mate for bed.

Amidst these ostentatious mechanisms,
We commence accustomed, rehearsed,
Preliminary probing game of gambits:

Yea, what's your name…?
How old are you?
Where are you from?
What shall I do for you?
How can I say this to you?
That I, I'm lost without you.
And really, I'm lusting for a mate.

You have suddenly stolen my reason.
And have tacitly cloned my thoughts.
So, shall I make bold to say this.
So, shall I manifest the core of love.
For you and to me now is the acceptable time!
Tomorrow and all what not, will be late.
I'll but peer into your sensual eyes.
If you permit, I'll convey that knowledge.
Depicting to the senses in colors.
The intensity of my passion in your favor.

Terms and conditions of contract are acknowledged.
Service Level Agreements dispatched and appreciated.
Proposal's presented right away but there's a problem:

"I must tell my mom,
Take you to my Pastor.
To certify all approvals."
Then harken.
This what I think,
Affection delayed is love denied.
Now is the auspicious moment.
Second chance is rarely common.
I'm fully poised now.

What else shall I say?
You've preferred charges against my offer:
"Love at first sight," you've called my gesture.
Yet dumbfounded I appeal this one more time.

Oblige me this promising encounter,
Deny not this entertaining affair.

III

"Since you insist, How else would I prove?
My system quakes knowingly.
Only you can quench this turbulence.
Dive in and swim.
The pool's warm and wet.
Breaststroke – your favorite start.
Scrub the walls with the strength of your man."

With persistent plodding on.
And ecstatic throbbing of hearts.
A denouement is climaxed.
Then the devastating revelation:
"I'm duly certified a carrier,
A transmitting agent,
Of the HIV-AIDS virus."
"What do you mean?
Why, I'm not been mindful.
Even to apply risk protection.
With the risk-laden sheath."

"What do you mean by what do I mean?
You mean to be violent; you want to strike my face?
You don't realize I'm a woman?"

"How do you mean; I don't know you're a woman?
Let me know; are you forgotten I'm a man?
It's just a few hours in the past.
Now it feels like ages ago.

Then, when we met,
Words were as soothing as balm.
Lips worked as swiftly as the magician's wand.
Your tongue as sweet as honey's taste.

Now filled with vile, as bitter as bile.
What a painful tale to tell!
What a cloud of burden to bear?
How shall we sell this tale?
To all that may care for caution.
And to folks who's got sex for auction.
We may never gain the realization.
Of where this has geared us.
Until we're totally deceived.
And we're utterly destroyed.
The deed is done.
The deal is on.
Let's carry it on.
Let's drag life forth.
Until next life up.
There we shall meet.
To part no more.

One Heart, One Soul

Dazzled in beauty.
In the innocence of fallow,
She stands in the halo.
Like un-mined goldmine
The heart of my heart.
Ever before the eyes of my mind.

At the outset of dawn.
By the onset of dusk.
Sooner or later,
She'll be here.
To sooth parched memories of the day.

I loved you at the first sight.
That accident of event.
Such incident of chance.
That proved the potency of your charm.
Your charm keeps me away.
So distanced from myself.
How soon it dawned.
You had left with a part of me.
When you departed from me.
And how I long now.

To have you,
Who for long was mine.
As I now realize,
The farther you are,
The more I'm convinced.
I'll not exist, isolated from you.
And cannot live,
Without your consoling presence.
Here am I.
In the body.
Away in mind.
Far away in thought.

You're not here with me,
I'm not there with you,
Yet you're always there for me.
I'm always here for you.
In the timeline of imagination.

The crawling pace of time hid you within
Until the season I'm grown to know.
And it's for the reason I'm truly matured.

Ever since that fire sparked off.
By that nature's event designed.
I'm being continually consumed.
With this passion of realization.
And this reality of revelation.
I had been half-baked without you.

Until we met,
I did not realize.
I was incomplete.
There's a trouble with the discovery.
I'm thrown into a gully of emptiness without you.

Now I long to see you.
I want to be with you.
To hold your lovely palm.
To smile into your unfailing face.
To admire your cheerful countenance.
To savor your alluring gait –
A minute spent without you,
Like million years in abyss of depression.

A day without you,
Like ageless devastation,
By tsunamis of loneliness.
Without you my inmost being,
Would be completely missing as in Adam's.

At night I tear at tears and curses,
For sweet dreams.
At daybreak I chew on sighs and hisses,
When I look round and you're not around.

Mumbling your name wets my lips.
Thinking about your fame breeds life.
Believing you're mine brings fortunes.

You're mine and I'm yours.

For that's what we are.

One Heart, One Soul in two bodies.

Book Two
Issues of Life

The Dancing Sun

The moon has come to the place it'll stay.
The cloud's in gloom like the rains will come.
We mourn like a people that have lost their hope.
The sun shines with a bright of its own.

With faith we trust the stars will save.
The day will start like a day that's great.
The sun appears like the moon it behaves –
To gaze at the sun is a thing that'll cost.

We stare at this, like the one that's a moon.
Had eclipse occurred I will not blink direct.
We dance and clap, we sing and smile.
We laugh and cheer an ovation with tears.

The sun is glad and dances and tumbles.
It struggles with the clouds and wriggles with the moon.
Our Lady and her son that dances with the moon,
Has struggled with the sun and partied with Angels.

The Missionary's Music
and Dance

I was growing and was going.

Do you know I was going and was growing.

And since I was growing, I had had some queries.

And for once needed some answers.

For some time, I sought tranquilizers.

What am I doing here; why am I here?

And where am I going?

And what is my mission and the rule of my life?

Then I heard the voice,

I am your maker.

And you're my worker.

Come to my presence in the high places.

And know my presents in high traces.

Then would I show to your senses,

That which will be your work.

And such which would rule your life.

I don't know your presence.

And have not heard of your presents.

For how long would I walk?

And for how long would we talk?
For seventy days and night shall you walk.
And seventy years and more shall we talk.

For that I have more questions and needed new answers
What should I carry or bring along for such a journey?
And who am I, that I should merit such a noble invitation?
Nor be considered for such a double indication.
Although I'm being exposed to a series of intimidation.
For which I fear to limit their limitations.
Fear not.
My rivers, springs, and forests
Shall provide for your worries.
Seven Rivers and seven Springs each shall you cross.
And traverse seven deserts and twenty-one forests.

What if your springs fail to yield their waters
And there be no honey in your forests,
Or the waters of your rivers be undrinkable.
And the peak of your mountains be too hot.
And the caves thereof and the valleys be too cold.
Or the deserts be somewhat too dry to sustain breathe.
Then would I perish in such a torturous journey.

Look here.
I have right now and right here:
Two calabashes of spring water,
Two gourds of domestic and wild honey,
Seven bags of tubers of yam
A whole measure of buffalo's hides
And a half measure of a leopard's skin

Three baskets of fried termites,
Two pouches of roasted locusts,
A two-year-old club and a freshly made spear.
A light and fire-emitting stone and this hammer,
A fairly used haversack,
All these and more,
Would I bring along for the journey.
For fear your own plan would fail.
Then would I have something to fall back on.

Then the Maker smiles and laughs.
What would all these do for a man,
For the journey of a lifetime?

Life's a Discovery

Life has some fair and dark stripes.

Lies have some flair to stir some doubts.

Has nature deigned the Blacks to strive?

To nurture feigned relevance in the scheme of strides?

Some Races are ordained with flairs to spot.

The strings to pull, and Nature would heal our wants.

They probe the crusts and explore the waves.

And stoke our trusts and excel in space.

We watch the sun in wonder how it be.

They latch onto the moon yonder their quest could reach.

We sulked and complained by the sea that we dread its depth.

They walked and explained on the seas as they traversed the earth.

We gaze in wonderment how the world runs the course of its
cause.
They blaze with unfolding discoveries about the universe we
own.
And return with amazing theories on how nature
operates our lives –
That below the seas; the earth, some gold and treasures hide
in mines.

Hard Times

Bought two dogs.
One's named Survival.
Another is called Hard Times.

Survival is pampered like a pet.
Fed with juicy meals like a pal.

Hard Times went in hunt for prey.
Fends for self like a yoked housemaid.

Not too long and Survival gave up the ghost!
I'm left with only Hard Times.
I've lost Survival, I've lost the instinct.
Deep fright seizes the man, left to strive with Hard Times.
The man engages Hard Times in a colloquy:

The world *intercourse* with men you're great.
"My worth diagnosed my mien I'm the worst;"
Do you believe that fear can kill like death?
"I did perceive that seers can seek my depths."
Did you conceive that the self can ruin the man?
"I did receive the gift from they that foretell."
Do you believe, like me you can fill the gap?

"My egos erode from the interiors of the past."
Do you believe you can fly like a bird in the air?
"I'm deceived; I'm damned from birth; I err?"
Do you admit that tears can heal like balm?
"I must confess that love can blind the sense."
Do you believe you can reign with kings someday?
"I recognize with luck a wren can sing on its day."

Even Hard Times has its day!
And even Tough Times has its own way.
Of…

How Do You Stop the Clock?

Like sitting by the riverside, watch a river flow,
How do you stop a river from its flow?
Like standing all morning watch the sun rise.
And lying all day admire it crawl across the sky,
And settle overhead and set at dusk,
How do you stop the sun from rising and setting?

Laziness! Have I ever offended you?
How do I stop the clock from ticking?
Somewhere, just somewhere out there,
Somehow, I just don't know where,
There's a gigantic clock ticking,
And counting at no cost our regrets –
The grudges we pile up.
Tick, tick, and tick,
The clock ticks rather loudly.

How do I stop the clock from ticking?
Tick, tick and she ticks again, all day.
How do I stop the three-pronged hand from moving?
Why do you keep so tirelessly busy?
Pushing my dreams beyond the reach of my ambitions.
How did you come about, oh! concept of time?

What can I do about it; it's too vast,
For my understanding to grasp.

Don't ask me why but I dread the idea of time.
Wish there were no time, no clock, and no seasons.
Then would I be at ease and even with the snail's pace,
I'd sure crawl to my destiny in earnest.

II

How do you expect to meet the dream tomorrow?
When you long to stop the clock,
The clock from its cycle?

Why do you want the clock still?
You hope you might run from the past?
As ugly with gloom like the back of night.
You fear it might catch up with you and explode?
The affairs you dread to reveal.
The things you're afraid you'd meet?

This grouse about time?
Don't ask me why dread I the clock,
Because I do.
The passion for passing shadows,
The fleeting realities I fail to acquire,
Make me real anxious.
As I had over the years watched,
My choicest desires flow past me in the present,
As I sat watching the past.
Blaming the times,
Cursing the seasons,

For the woes I claim to be mine.
The past is past; gone for good.
The future belongs to all who refuse to look back,
And linger in the past,
Move ahead with the clock as it ticks.
Forgotten that woman?
She's named Lot's wife.
Why would time not leave us behind as a pillar of failure?
When we look back and dwell on the past, long gone?

How do I stop the clock from running?
Why do I want her stopped, anyway?

The times are past; the seasons are gone.
Yet we remain in one spot marking time.
That's why we want the clock stopped?

Quite impossible!
For I'd rather stop myself
From reaching the promised land.
How do I stop the times and the seasons?
I'll keep busy with my mind and with my hands.

How do I stop the clock from its rulings?
Interpreting the lots that are yet to be?
By offending laziness of course.
Laziness!
I'm going to offend you now!
I'll work.
Work and work again,
And again, I'll work.
And like that, either stop the clock,
Or move in swift accord with time.

III

Kill time? What is time?
Some say they just want to kill time.
How can you kill the clock?
Because the clock is the time.
And with all the "killings" done her by idle men,
Time still lives on.
She moves on still.

How do we stop the clock from moving?
For the day we stop the clock,
Is the way our woes and miseries shall end.
Failures will cease and there'll be nothing but void.
Then why should you stop the clock?

Weathering the Storm of Fate

Like a search for a needle in a haystack
Was the question of the part taken by fate,
In weathering this storm in the drama of life.
Until I came to the Goldsmith's workshop,
To gain some understanding in good faith,
Of how I'd been a victim of unfair judgment,
As the former harmers viciously.
Deforming, forming, and reforming,
The heated metal, I pondered.
How hatefully you dare, I wondered.
Pounding so harshly on the "hated" metal.
And how helpless the melted piece
Seemed now, hapless for the merited peace.
So ill-treated and shattered at will.

Though precipitated on this need for jewels, I guess.
Or perpetrated in the extreme greed for ornaments.
Would I compromise this disgust?
At this labored pressure.
Nor could Such treasured quest justify,
This measured threat,
To so Natural a leisured state deserving.
No sooner had he lowered that masterpiece.

That had gleefully emerged from his mastery.
Then his song of fulfillment in chimes:
No toil, no spoil; no tests, no rest.
A precious ornament highly priced
By the beauty merchants that are on the rise!
Which in turn will trade-off for a prize.
Than the veil fell off my sight.
And had I had the sway.
I would trade my man away.
For the prized tourist's treasure.
Only then did I realize with a measure of ease.
I am a pencil in the hands of fate.

Not Yet at Ease

You are unknown to me.
Since I know not your habitation.
Nor the how to your dwelling.
Yet none of these do I seek.
For it's your selfsame prompting and preoccupation –
You're proposing to visit me with your unfolding.
And though I am ignorant of the hour or the day.
I know for certain you shall come someday.

With the pace of a snail, you move progressively.
With the certainty of daybreak, you arrive effectively.
And with such persistent efficiency,
You advance with efficacy.

Bringing the Maker's blueprint.
Which I know not, though I console in this:
I know of him who knows you.
The one that governs your doings.

The one that decrees the nature of the end,
From the beginning.
Oh, the future! My own future!
Oh, my tomorrow in the days to come,

Oh, my lots in the scale of time,
My portion in the allocated events on course.
And my place in the frame of History.
What have you got in store for me?
What are you bringing to restore to me?
What would I leave behind when I'm gone?

Where shall I be when you come?
For now, I get the fright of my life.
Eaten up by worries and fear,
Beaten up by uncertainties and doubts,
For the way you handle my destiny.
For today you treat her so lackadaisically.
And as if she were not fragile.
And as such, would I say I trust you not?

Do I lack confidence in your mission?
Do I doubt the authenticity of your influence?
Anxiety presumes I've been.
Because you clap the Maker's plan so closely to your heart.

Would that I could merely peep.
Would that I could look into your hands,
To behold that which you bear.
Whether it is of good or bad news.
Whether it is of good or evil report.
Then could I be at ease.

I'm so unsure from my quest.
That I'll be so secure at least.
By that which you'll bring at last.

For that, I resign my will to Him.

The one I say I know who knows you.

The one who governs all your deeds.

With a hope designed but unsteady.

He has already assigned and apportioned to me.

A unique mission in life.

As I wait in this patient hope.

You'll come with the tomorrow of my wish.

Questions for Life

There's been this on-going battle within.
I'm afraid they could be more than one man in me.
For I could see more than four nations at war.
Peradventure, there are more than three natures in man.

That nature which I know not, I see.
But there's another and the other one.
They're hidden from me and the public.
Although there's yet another.
That's known to some and all.

Mommy tell me; daddy let me know.
Where was I before the two of you met,
Before you both acquired the marital congruence.
Was this according to the rule of nature?
Who am I?
What was I?

If retrospection were gained.
With the fusion of human elements learned.
Where am I from?
Where's my destination?
Mommy tell me; daddy let me know.

How did we three meet?
Where did these three meet?
Was it on the winding path?
That winding path to the stream of struggles?
Was it on the bumpy road of toils and labor?
Was it in the forest of fortunes and treasures.
Was it on a bed of roses and pleasures?
Rid of thorns and prickles?
My present fortunes lend no such support.
That I had a silver spoon then in my mouth.

Was I a weakling in the bout?
In the battle for survival,
Among the most fitted in the struggle.
My current stature suggests none.

Why then am I not counted,
Counted in the meantime.
Among the highs and the creams of the earth.
Among the nobles, the great men of the world?

Was there thunderclap or sunshine?
Was the surroundings serene or ethereal?
Was the climate humid, stifling, or gloomy?
I want to know if the weather was dry, cloudy, or clear.
"Why do you ask?
Why do you want to know?
Curiosity killed the cat."
Was Mom's immediate admonition.
As always, would swiftly adjure.
Had you known Inquisitiveness,

Would you own to open up?
Inquisitiveness is the mother of inventions.
The second agent of adventures.

Tell me my yester years,
And I'll tell you now,
How our tomorrow shall be.

"Ask your father."
Was Mom's second attempt.
To circumvent the matter.
Or to parry the answer.
"Your father seems to know it all."

What kind of star did appear in the sky?
Since you know exactly when I was born.
Did you find out from the gods?
What was to govern me on the earth?
And be the rule of my life and my work?

"I did not observe.
I had no courage to ask."
Was Mom's final echo.

Why therefore did you decide?
On this name which I bear?
With all these same things which I hear?
Since you never cared to enquire.
For my star could've starred in the clouds.
And zodiac could've featured in the heavens.

For a man's nature is in his name.
And failure to understand his nature is his bane.
A man's deeds are dictated by the same.
His fortunes are governed by his frame.
What you called me, I now bear as a name.

Did you consult him who bid me into your womb?
Or religiously consider on your honor,
The circumstances of my birth?
While deciding the stuff I would be made of.
Predicated upon this name you gave me?
Whether you know it or not,
That is a question of spilt milk.
Yet what I am today
Is what you gave me to be.

Nature's Course of Course

One-on-one, I must tell you,
Left to me, you ought to know.
Man's greed's insatiable indeed.
Nature's groomed enough for man's need.

And sometimes when he is far
From dreams attained at par
For want of proper initiative, he takes
Or there's been prompt detour from the stakes,
Since he's on the wrong road, so required
Saddened by the saddle of throng of loads so acquired.
He feels devastated in retrospect of this,
Divine fill of disappointment expressed and borne.
And long before, the road will lead to naught.
The longings are for the roosts that will breed in the north.
He feels cheated by Nature and its order.
And ill-treated by comparison with others.
Wherefore nurtures grief and mumbles.
For so many endeavors so immature jumbles
Justifiably too, he plans so elaborately to grumble.
That Nature's been so callously unfair to some.

Cry of the Motherless

Dear mother, here's a world.
Great mother, there is war.
I hear that in that other world,
Where they claim is where you're,
In its very fullness they now tell there's love.
And if it be so as I hear,
Why did mother leave me here?

And if it were not so as I believe,
Great woman, where then are you?
Were it so well with your soul,
Lovely mother would come for me.
Great woman though you come not,
Beloved one, oblige me this one.
A single and only one question,
Which I know that you will know:

Why's my own mortal world so wicked and so inhuman?
Fright-stricken, not for your absence,
Scared I am of the human race.
Their very own, their own excuse of real weaknesses
As they are wont to foreclose my reeled witnesses
Is that I'm blind in mind, in thought, and in will.

Phlegm becomes my milk, dear mother I'm hungry.
Ceaseless flow of tear's my water, great woman, I'm thirsty.
Here I am alone, not so lonely, you must know.
Painfully but gainfully pre-occupied am I,
Right here with a world.
With that world, that very real world,
Of my own choice – that's my world.

A world where men would hate themselves less savagely.
A world where men would be less wicked and barbaric.
A world where men would treat womanhood less carelessly.
A world where people would handle the motherless, less an outcast.
A world where people would be less engaged in deadly competitions.
A world less frequently involved in armed struggles and conflicts.

The only sound I hear in this part is gunshots –sounds of annihilation.
I can also inhale the smell of gunpowder in East Greenwich.
And clatters of swords near the Equator.
Generated by men who claim they know.
Propagated and advanced by civilized neo-barbarism.
Marked by these massive roaming of dead bodies.
That's defied these invasive swarming of countless hungry vultures.
Besides these numberless bodies honored in mock burials,
Like this grave close to the cave where I live,
Which's sure to house triple five scores,
Of putrefied bodies purified with formaldehyde.

As I live with these and dead, my sole companions.
A tense and subsistent dread created by this thirst for blood,
Has become my conscious heartbeat,
And like my implosion, the world's been turned
Into a molecular time-bomb pending explosion.
Anywhere I look, I see hatred at work.
Whenever they open their mouths, I hear bitter strife at war.
When they laugh, what I see is mockery at nature.
And whenever they cry, I find greed and ingratitude.
Mingling down with tears of insatiability.
Therefore, I think of a world where men would be less greedy.

Whenever it be, I'm sure to touch off,
On the people's premeditated ridiculed abuse.
Every angle I look, I see intimidations and jeers.
As they pride themselves on my beggarly destitution.
And pleasure in my downcast disposition.
Taking delight in the mockery of my fate.
They curl their lips in derogation as they learn.
Of my "un-noble" birth and are acquainted,
With my "ignoble" nativity.
For they're wont to sneer at my color.
And they're sure to smear my reputation.

They shake their head in ridiculed pity.
On learning the place of my birth.
Which's been condemned to rubbish.
In deep-seated and ageless bias.
As all the good and beauties,
Which had been just acknowledge of me,
Has now been swallowed up in this discovery,

"Can anything good come out from a colored man?"
Would be simple and without qualms,
Summarize this ancient verdict.

And for this alone and other causes,
Father's gone off to the forests and mountains.
To sing and feed on the music of birds and reptiles.
I'll soon be gone to the rivers and streams.
To clap and dance with the fishes and lilies.
Peradventure, we find knowledge from among
The birds and fishes – knowledge the mother,
Of all motherhoods, cradle of all wisdom.
Within these we find some fulfillments.
Beyond them, we hope to find a home.

Why Do We Fear Death?

I'm afraid of death; definitely, I will die.
Nobody wants to die, but certainly, we shall die.
I'm killed by fear, but not really for what I know.
Uncertainties and despair; are what ruined me once and for all.
When death knocked at my gate, I wanted to tell it to wait awhile.

We are killed by fear; no one wants to die,
Definitely, we shall die, for certainty, we shall die,
Inevitably man must die, just one and not again,
To be killed not by fear alone,
For fear alone has ruined my world,
And hopelessness has ruled my days.

We are afraid of death; why should we not die?
Definitely, we shall die; however, so long before we die,
However so old, death is death.
But now I'm so young; death is death.
Just one day and not again; definitely, all shall die,
Definitely…

If and Then...

If black is a curse and white the cause.

Then blank is the page of rationality in a God that's white.

If a pest fixed pies in the past,

Then its taste lists lies in the cast.

If the bulk lifts a tool and dies,

Then luck befits a pool of dice.

If a kith licks his kin like a broth,

Then the mouse clicks and nibbles like a crook.

If a thief runs away with the loots,

Then our chief grunts with harps and lutes.

Then our land wakes with hopes and heals.

If the lost takes all the dope on his heels.

And if the thief never comes back to steal the wealth,

Then the land rests in bliss from the West.

The Victor's Song

For ages unknown, folks have got this to say.

For every cause known, there's a price to pay.

And for any effect, there must be a cause to start

Men who know this never from their lofty course defect.

Not a few are well aware again:

There's no gain without pain.

There's no rest without test.

There's no best without zest.

There's no spoil without toil.

No omelets before eggs are brought.

No victory before battles are wrought.

No victor without a vanquished.

No reaper without a Sower in the past.

No crown without a cross at par.

The Nobles and the Miserables[2]

The journey of life begins like that.
The echoes of it reverberate at last.
That however, a pond befits.
There's bound a mighty crab to fit.

There's a city of the nobles.
And there's a community of *miserables*.
The one's basking in a temporal phase of glory,
For he's held in the highest wave of esteem.
The others regarded with the basest scorn,
And's spurned.
There's nothing attractive about him.
In this sensual order.

One's born on a day when all's gone,
To the labor in toils, the farms and on tours.
As mother's left in lonely pains of labor.
And with this configuration in place.
He's discharged into the earth to strive.
With the lonely world of solitary sobriety.

---

[2] This form is used here to establish harmony of sounds and syllable.

As all's calm and recollected in space.
And the odds high and repositioned in folds.

Another's brought forth on a day,
In his case, folks are all gathered around the woman,
In pangs of pain so joyfully engaged around the medics.
And with such configuration so associated,
He's heralded into the waiting embrace,
Of cheers and ovations and celebrations.
For this earth-coming of a new mortal.

Contaminated in spirit and soul.
With such noisy formation for a present.
With silver spoon in their mouth.
They ride through life in the crests,
Of noisy commotion and arrogance.

This one is born into an Eden of comforts and myths.
Destined to a fall by the allurements of his niche.
Crippled in mind and thought by riches.
His perception of reality transcends,
No more than four walls of sensual senses.
As they live in oceans of wealth.
And depart the world pauperized.
For there's nothing left to their name.
Their magnificent mansions and luxurious estates,
Leave no trace of them in the books.
Some of these and the rest,
Who are of the noble parentage,
Turns out the *miserable*, in fact.
Because of their imbecility.

Then those few who're just
Of your kind of miserable birth,
Are churned out the nobles of the world.
Their senses transcendentally illumined.

That one's brought forth into a manger of circumstance.
Bereft of all comforts and mirth.
To whom a spirit of holy solitude,
And creative imagination is endowed.
To the other, a spirit of naughty arrogance,
And intuitive waywardness is bestowed.
Who go through life in fear of death,
For they die fearing to leave their acquired vanities.
For the realities which they fear to face,
When the roll will be called in ages to come.

The *miserable* builds castles with bare hands.
But no one ever notices his presence.
Hence, he passes through the world unsung.
Nor anyone willfully willing to reward his labors.
Yet the *miserables* re-make visible world.
While living in the unseen waves sublime.

When you kill their body in brutal tortures,
They begin to live in blissful vitality,
For they live dying for others and the rest.
And they die to live forever in rest.
For when all things are gone and lost.
Only one thing shall remain at last –
The immortal works of a mortal man.

Better to Be Late Than "The Late"

The bout for life is about relief.

To live like flies is to risk grief.

We perch like flies from places like pests.

In search of wants, we're wont to haste.

The need to trace our choices we waste.

The race itself is a bit for self.

For once at a rate, I stake myself.

To take the war at a pace that's base,

And drive the sword like a brute is worse.

The time will come, and I'll own my dreams.

And now it's early to wail I'm weak.

For then, it's late to wait for the best.

I'll fight again till I bet my last.

And will count my gain till I take my rest.

Book Three
The Affairs of Men

Mama Africa ... Still Groping In Darkness

Wake up! Get up! The sun will soon be up.
And leave us behind these resonating chambers.
Of snores and slumber at the dawn of morn.
At that dawn, we acted out that it'll never be dusk.
Then the night came, and we thought as we now think,
That there'll never be light of dawn again,
We still look for cause in the transient effects of cause.
We still champion the course of the downward regress of our
course.
To the realization of the end for which all flesh are made.
But how long shall we wait for things to change?
And not work long for the change to things?

Get up! Get up! Rise up and gird your loins,
While the centuries and the ages are yet to come
For sooner than later as the centuries and the years run by
They shall come back to find you still sitting in darkness.

Mama Africa's failures are no more poverty of knowledge,
Lack of ideas or poverty of materials as of mental
enslavement.
Mama's lack of wisdom about nature, cause, and effects
And the interpretations thereof caused an ageless building-up
of thick darkness inside her.
Her loss of contact with the Arts cost her her civilization.
Now the woman who prided herself as the mother of
civilization
Murdered in the heat of the resistance against robbery and
debauchery.
Africa is still new, too close to the jungles of her primate days!

Why have you constituted these monumental failures?
And nonentity in all fields of nature,
Groping along this tortuous tunnel,
That leads into the dark of your early beginnings.

All down the ages, life has situated us,
In treasure Islands without labor, or
Our trading the highlands for treasures
The years and the days, the times and the seasons,
Have run their cycles.
Yet we've remained on the same spot of the circle.
Glorying in pristine equivocation,
Singing our *"Credo"* in another man's tongue.
How long shall we remain in this armchair of indolence?
Crying over the spilled milk of our ugly past and memories,
Of slavery, colonialism, and imperialism,
Which crept in and stole the peace of the moment,
And like the sun advanced forth upon a land unknown.

The path ahead is as dark as ever,

Because the Africa of this age's been further blinded,

By the dazzling light of western civilization which betrays
this darkness.

For this darkness does not comprehend the light within her.

Day by day, year by year through the centuries,

She faces suspicion, intimidation, humiliation,
misrepresentation, misinterpretation,

And downright rejection.

To remain ignorant of these unfolding schemes,

In this supreme journey to the common end of all things,

Is to grope in darkness.

Look within you, Africa; you will find answers to all things.

Over Population

When the hall's hurled with bullies,
And the park craned with pulleys,
Even the heirs will perish like flies.

When the fattest that lands produce,
And the latex that fangs induce,
Bundled in one accord and delivered,
Blended with what we want and need,
Given that our hands idle away with ease,
Even then, shall our greed advance in swarms.

When the land overflows with milk and honey,
And the pilgrims inflow without limits of numbers,
Even then shall some natives lack their due.

When the eggs in women breed in leaps,
And the cringes in men's walls increase their bonds,
Even then shall our wants increase in bounds.

When we hide in caves for the hail to cease,
And we lie in waves with men and women alike; we seize.
Even then, shall hell rain the ruin we dread.
When the house is filled with men and women,

In their numbers until they're numberless,
And the walls painted with darkness like colors of night,
Even then shall boys and girls roam the streets, motherless.

Cry of the Childless

I'm coming into the world,
To be in the league of things,
To take part in the wing
Assigned me to control and wheel.

Here I am now in the mien.
Miffed with no story to tell.
Have played more than 60 matches.
With no scores to yell!

Now the folks confront me,
With questions of my nature –
A wonder at my state.
"You're meant to be a woman.
You've never wooed any man.
To place you among we men.
To gather the fruits from the forests.
To perpetuate and control the forecasts."

Right now, at this new dawn
There's yet no cry of the new one.
To announce at least for once
I have a relevance of a woman.

In the final game I played
I was sure I'm a winner.
I was strong and tough at least.
Spared no tactics and technique at all.
Lo! and behold I've lost in it again!
Twelve and score months have since gone.
Yet the story swiftly remains same.

Had I run in the wrong track?
Would I be content with this loss?
Yet I followed the rules of the game.
Disqualification was again the gain.

Who's it that distributes these things?
Come forth with my own gift of children!
Or step forth to resolve this rift.
The raging battle among my lovers and boyfriends.

The household of Opobo.
Oloibiri and Ughelli, Koko and Okpei,
Bonny and Segema, Brass and Oleh,
Have never known peace since that day,
The day I was diagnosed to be pregnant from nature.
The descendants of Urhobo and Ogoni,
The daughters and sons of Itsekiri, Ijaw, and Isoko,
Have been in perpetual crises – a few years thereafter:
For their sons and daughters, I've been barren in practice.

Who says I'm to be blamed?
Doctor! Doctor! Come, confirm.
Was this not your report?

Written in your own ink and with your mark?
That I'm fertile and laden with possibilities?
Then my futile measures to prove as reported?
The only voice I hear now is miscarriage.

Who's miscarrying what?
Is it I? The midwives or who?
Sixty and some years on top.
I remain childless, not a case of stillbirth!
Look at menopause!

Menopause stares in my face.
It's now crawls forth,
For when all my ova have run out,
Shall no quantity of sperm count
Rewind the hand of time,
To bring back these years of wastes.
In memory of the days of the spoils.

Bring Back Those Days!

The First time we're Talking…
I remember a poem.
A poem we read in Senior Secondary three
Or was it in Junior Secondary?
It was in High School, though.

This First time we're Talking…
I remember David Diop, the Poet.
He reminds me of "the VULTURES".
And the first lines come to my mind:
IN THOSE DAYS…

I remember Nigeria.
The first man comes to mind.
Mr. Present President!
And all recent Presidents!!

One of the soldier-bloody-civilian-turned presidents,
Come to the fore,
As ASO ROCK is evoked to the core,
And THEIR promises rush to the mind.
As our memory dances around the past
And recalls a Poem written in 2006.

At the NYSC orientation camp in Nwangene,
Nwangene, a rusty town in Imo State, Nigeria.

Lo! and behold,
The First time we're Talking…
First line comes to mind.
IN THOSE DAYS…

In those days…
when civilization built up,
When Europe and America were winding up
Operation and handing down politics to the Natives.
When Agriculture was the mainstay of Nigeria's economy.
Reinforced with Oils and gas, the wealth flowed.

In those days…
When visiting Malaysian scientists
Took back Nigeria's Oil palm seeds.
Now they're the largest exporter of oil palm in the world.
The First bell rings in my mind.
Bring back THOSE DAYS!

Bring back THOSE DAYS.
When I could turn on a WC in the underdeveloped
Old city of Abakaliki in Anambra State.
One of the LGAs in that old State.
And water could rush around from somewhere.
To the amazement of a kid.
Clear the debris deposited a while ago!
No! It's not used water from doing the dishes.
Nor the black water from rinsing clothes.

No! It's not the red water from the dirty well in the yard; the
case today.

The heart yearns:
Bring back THOSE DAYS.

Bring back those days Mr. President!
A piece written in 2006 in Nwangene[3]
in memory of a retired General –
His stewardship as Mr. President.
Has followed you Mr. President on Facebook
And when your thinking is considered.
Only one thought besieges the mind.
The Joker in The Rock.
Then the only cry that's left on our lips is:
BRING BACK THOSE DAYS!

---

[3] See The Joker in the Rock in this collection

Unemployment

Lured out of despondence with jumbo claims,
All we like the white stork migrate to your farm.
We crawled on land to a distance with time,
That compels a glide on the skies to arrive,
Occupied with revived hope we would now survive –
Sapped of access to modern means to move, we persist,
And trudged on in hope you'll keep your word,
And keep our hands busy as you'd regularly claimed.
We struggled to keep back vituperations and grudges,
And defied the wet clouds laden with rains and storms,
We embraced the hot skies that outwitted the rains and shines,
And approached your courts in honor to your biddings,
We expended hard-earned means that we scarcely afford –
Eked out from hard-fasts on meals and necessities,
And sacrificed what we lacked to arrive at your farms.

We arrive at your farms to be engaged in a way,
Only that we're dismayed at your obligatory absence.
Did you not know we're coming as you said?
There's no one behind to receive our worries.
Except for the few nomadic tradesmen with queries,
Who're more than prepared to bleed your guests –
Some of your guests would dare need relief:

"How much is pure water, how much for your popcorn?
How much for ice cream; how much for peanuts?"
Would price embarrassing declaration of costs,
Per unit means of assuaging those scourging torments of
hunger and thirst.
With nowhere to wedge our weary frames.
Procured at such highly skyrocketed hike in price,
We played to the mercy of these opportunistic nomadic
shylocks.

We endured all but this psychological devastation,
With despair wrought, fraught with tears of gloom:
Your bloated promise of jobs,
Is but a phantom flaunt.

This Kind of Color

What pattern of trends these we see?
These bandits that glut on the wealth,
Of United Peoples of the Nations,
Gloating around the earth in shameful garbs,
Grabbed by guilt.
Guilt acquired as a response to failure,
Failure to preserve safety of nature as we know it.

This kind of color's never seen in purity.
The color of evil procured with impunity.
Of dead conscience and perilous days.
Of wicked passions and depraved ways.
Of a religious ideology that glories in terrors.
Obscure schemes networked in errors of judgment.
Bizarre violence and wanton deaths.
Manifested in selfish sacrifice of selves,
Procuring death of one in public,
For the extermination of the rest at hand.

The colors of nuclear games of hide and seek.
Carried in mutual suspicion with tricks.
The color of sheer greed for domination,
The colors of wars and shared destiny for all,

Of culpability of United Nations in blames.
Of common drift of the world to anarchy and flames.
Subsumed in maniacal implosion of hunger and thirst.
Hunger or thirst for extra-territorial dominance that's shriveled the world.
The globe's now a molecular time bomb at last,
That's now pending explosion at the blast of egos.

The Church Warden's Dilemma

Ever been in tragedy you want to cry,
Tears rolled in comedy you run to inquire,
Laughter's for comedy; tears run at tragedy.
Yet none of these he's got turned a remedy,
For these and others, apprehend this dilemma,
In the Cathedral of the holy mountain of God,
On this occasion, the holy farewell to honors,
This glorious exit of the Supreme Head in colors.

Seated in the midst of the holy pews,
Reserved for his kinds, the holy few,
A messenger of the gods is spotted.

But lo! He's in a posture posed,
Just for the weak and the tired.
Hands restful on the pews, head-charged knees,
Just one duty discharged as he kneels.
How do you prove duly as in this stupor could?
Be well, attuned to the highest frequency of gods.
The guilt of non-performance of function.
The prick of conscience for dereliction.
The embarrassment for wrong premise of motif.
The guilt of conscience, the conscience of failure.

The failure of zeal; the zeal of innocence.
The innocence of reason, reason soiled with ignorance,
Championed in a psychosomatic siege.
Laid by these gods in man's attire.
Who, never wrong in doings,
Ascribe theocratic manifestation to whims and arrogance.

With fear and trembling like oil.
Against sticky background in toil.
He migrates to the site of the sighted disgrace.
Against the will of the other voice in regrets.
With the warden's wand likewise wavers.
With apprehension of possible misapplied sense of duty.
Nudges his elbow, *"sit up, Father"*.

The revered Father looks up, cuts off,
Drooling saliva from mouth.
And wipes up reddened eyes,
That's drooping with drowsiness.
And braces up pale face,
That's dulled with wearisomeness;
With grimace shot missiles at target.
With bushy eyebrows intimidates the Warden:
"How dare you interrupt,
This divine missive glowingly in flows?
Couldn't you see I'm meditating?"

Our Slave Masters

These two are still our slave masters.
Till this day,
Religion is politics, as politics is in religion.
Politics is a religion as practiced in a region.
Religion is politics, and politics is a religion.
Unlike oil mingled with water, the two are miscible.
If religion is good, then politics is good.
But *"politics is not good",* so religion is not good.
If politics is a tool, then religion is a farm.
Actually, religion is a tool and oppression is the quest.
All Religions pray to a kind of a god.
Hawks, predators, scavengers represent this God –
And they prey on their good subjects.
And religion becomes worse than politics.

The Way of All Tyrants

What type of culture are we got?

What manner of governance are we seeing?

In these bandits glutting themselves on our resources.

Gloating around in shameful garbs of guilt.

Acquired as a response to failure,

To do what's undertaken on oath.

And what manner of people are these?

Whence do they come from?

They're evil with impunity:

Their consciences are dead.

Their conducts are perverse.

Their ways are deprave.

Their languages are obscene.

Their deeds are cunning.

Their wealth is questionable.

Their quest is unquenchable.

Their wisdom is base.

Their mouths are filths.

Their thoughts are ill.

Their deeds are evil.

Their hands are full of blood.

Their ends are surely at hand.

What manner of culture is this?
A culture that glorifies evil.
A culture that looks down on sweat.
A culture built on obscure scheming.
Upon demonic maneuvers and bizarre practices.
A culture that beautifies evil.
And cloths sin with saintly garbs.
A culture created by social craftiness blinded by ignorance.

A culture of ostentation and pretention.
That honors laziness and rewards mediocrity.
A culture that is purely alarming.
A culture that is surely unbecoming.
Practiced and worshipped,
By a people destined to unassuming end.
What shall I say about their end?
Their end shall be like a voyage on sea.

All journeys are laden with risks of a kind.
Their endeavors are labeled with tricks of the mind.
But their end, like one billed for termination,
Upon the high seas shall come at once,
Like the gloaming upon a city.
For though they die upon "treasures" and pleasure.
Wine, dine, and song with their immoral women,
On their laps and with their mortal lips
Contaminated with dyes from lipsticks.
They die the most miserable sort of death.
For on confirmation of the cheering news as fresh.
The masses advance into the streets, in droves.
In celebration of the departure of a beast.

It's only then will they realize like Nebuchadnezzar.
They'd been a lonely sort of miserable being.

Their inheritances are a mockery.
To be gambled with by foes.
Their funerals are frightful.
Attended?
Attended only by deprave sons and daughters.
Their mourning is done alone by them.
At the last minutes of departure,
Full of regrets.
Full of uncertainty to destinations unknown.

For they hear music of intimidation.
Scared of venturing forward.
Frustrated by inordinate instincts.
Projected by egoistic pleasures.
Retracted by ignominious ambitions.
Rejected by History, rejected by the gods.
Dejected at death, ejected by the world.
Haunted by retribution, evicted by family and friends.
So then, the road becomes murky and rough.

For nothing shall be left to their memory.
For the folks shall snap their fingers.
At the mention of their name.
In a bid to dissociate themselves,
With the kind of fate that'll befall them.
And absolve themselves from this type of end:

"May I have nothing to do with your linage.
And be never linked to your kind of language.

"May the evil that men do live with them.
May he who beats the drums of death,
Dance the dance of perpetual funeral.
May they that slay the innocents with power,
Be betrayed from within their household,
Slain by their own daughter.
May they compete over their wives in bed,
With their own sons, kith and kin.

"May they be buried by thunder.
Transported to the great beyond in high seas.
May their soul not miss road,
In its journey to pains and torments.
"May sounds of laughter be heard,
In the neighborhood at their death.
May the neighbors break into dancing,
And merry-making for a time and a time,
Like slaves whose freedom has come unannounced."

Epilogue

The Days of the Grand Rebellion

The silence shall be as awesome and ominous as the depth of
abyss.
As an awfully strange day meets with vicissitudes of life.
Expectant maidens shall bleed out their fetuses.
In natural abortions and abortive miscarriages.
Nursing parents shall forget when it's time,
That the time is ripe to water-feed babies on their laps.
Suckling mothers shall forbid neonates to lap their nipples.
Orchards shall swallow up their yields and fruits –

Farms and gardens ate up their produce.
Blossoming fructifying plants gave up tender fruits.
Budding flowering crops let go of immature pollen grains.
And the honeycombs failed to produce honey.

Boys and girls will stand naked and watch in shock.
Clutching at their innocent organs in palms as they watch,
dismayed.
Women shall bear their breasts to the setting sun to protest
and curse.
Men shall hiss and embrace distress with grunts – fraught with
regrets.
Maidens shall curse the day when the first man,

For the first time ate the fruit, forbidden as it is.
And the first woman forfeited her virgin state as it stood.
Men shall sing dirges, and women chant abusive name-calling.
Against the earth, the universe, and their elements.
Young men shall render war chants and
Boys plus girls shall rub their eyes in anxiety.

Dogs shall hide their tails behind their legs in fear.
Or they shall refuse to wag their tails for fear of the state of things.
Livestock shall refuse to graze in lands with lush and green vegetations.
They shall neither graze in the verdant fields nor in their stalls.
Nanny goats shall declare a fast and decline from chewing the cuds.
And cattle shall refrain from mooing and booing as they fight with cold.
Rodents shall stay back in their Burrows and hide in crevices.
As they embark on a stay-at-home hunger strike,
Birds, afraid of erring the pensive mood of the day,
Shall fail woefully to fly across the sky and the clouds.
Nor would they sit to brood eggs and young birds in nests.
All plants and vegetations shall refuse to move their hands and feet.
Even as the wind stands still in total submission and apprehension of this day.

The Joker in The Rock[4]

Crouched in the pouch blest,
He rode to the cradle crest,
Bestrode onto the saddle fixed,
And ruled with clenched fists.

As he coils with drenched bosom,
Smiles as cherished dreams blossom.
Casts a gaze upon fortunes flourished,
Glances past the dazed folks famished,
Would remember his days of embrace with shackles locked,
A memory that would merit him more cackles.

As he watched the people perish in numbers,
Assemblymen latched onto the vaults in slumbers,
Assembled without the polling counts mattered,
As robbery at the polling booths is mastered.

While elemental sense of responsibility diminished.
Incremental sort of hardship in the land diffused,
Began him, his rehearsed comedy,
In a business less requiring this remedy.

---

[4] As used here is symbolic of Nigeria's seat of power (Government)

"Up, up to the theatre you go.
Gather the masses for the fiesta of jokes.
Garner the media for the fiats online.
Table the scripts to the experts on-rolls.
While I wait at the studio for the augmented speech."

Seated in a well-rehearsed posture thrust.
Like a boxer in a duel poised, struts.
As he sat in that practiced position pressed.
Would you wonder what animal so much stressed?
Like a chimpanzee from the zoo into the screen broke.
Or another baboon from wild into tame brought.

Then in his ridiculed jest spurn,
Cast a glance at the bedraggled masses,
Bedraggled in poverty and in want,
And it would dawn on his mind in wonder,
There's too much drums of pleasure in this land,
There'd be much more measures of austerity.
Meted out and ensure there's not a splinter of leisure.
Remnant on the people's stifled menial life.

"Patience, patience, fellow country people.
Sacrifice, sacrifice, timid complaining patriots.
No more idle stories,
That'll cost our sovereign nation,
Her history as a country.
Bid me eat the fill of my heart.
Perhaps there might be crumbs,
From this dynastic banquet thrust,
Then would your patience trump."

But for how long shall we wait?
Year after year, day after day.
Our hopes are blown away,
Into a future that may never come,
A future borne on bare lips,
On the lips of self-imposed marauders.
Who're bereft of the wherewithal,
It'd take to envision the imaginary tomorrow,
Though with excess cruel artistry,
They simulate same:

A future built on flaked promises,
And hinged on fake hopes,
A future that flouts us into the empty space
Of backwardness and regression.
Designed to space us as far apart in numbness,
In numbness of mind and thought as per reasoning,
Lest we like the Eaglet among the chicks strayed,
Come to our senses and realize.
And realize we ought to be soaring and orbiting,
the space of modernism and industrialized world.
Rather than scavenging in this debris of Stone Age.
How long shall we sing these dirges?
For how long shall we feed from refuse dumps?
What else shall we sacrifice:

The sweat of our harsh labors.
The price of our ignorance.
The zeal of our youth.
The strength of our grayed and strained hairs.
Acquired as shock from oppression as collective heirs.

The pains of losses of our collective gains.
Looted amidst wasted years of woes,
Roasted in vanities of self-pursuits by foes,
The clatter of our empty dishes.
The luster of our self-will to survive.
Independent of the gains of our collective inheritance,
So cruelly deprived us?
The blood of our coffins.
The bones of the graves of our perished kith and kin,

Buried in the abyss of deprivation and wants,
In the woes of our years of wasted Opportunities,
And squandered treasures in the booms of the seventies.
Our tears over the spilled milk,
Of our traded values and fortunes,
Reminiscing memories of the good old days –
Of decent and cherished livelihood,
Versus this recent and merited preference
For those yester years,
Lost to the past by mindless squandermania.
As senseless idiots, mediocre and thoughtless actors,
Besieged the theatres of power –

Gained only as a narration from
Those who went before us marked in vantage with age,
Whose only edge over us is their age.
For its only here that folks remain fools at forty.

And when shall this endless wait end?
When shall we cease this countless count of losses?
And resume a ceaseless count of our cherished gains?
Or when shall tears dry off our wrinkled faces?

How long shall these tears roll past our crinkled cheeks?
And for how long shall we continue to feed
Those who want it so,
Who pleasure in them:
With this pressure of the scramble,
For those his taunted crumbs –
Our gloomy countenances and long faces.
Our empty stomachs and hungry outlooks.
Our unkempt bodies and haggard looks.
Our bursting fury and doubled frustration.
Our dumped ego and banished psyches.
Our blooming expectations and dashed hopes.
Our muted grumbling and rooted mumbling.
Our crippled will and diseased frames.

About the Book

The last few decades have been so uncharacteristically defined and challenging to people of all nations that only a few would disagree that the universe needs to look at itself and review its relationship with the nations that make up the globe. People become so restless-footed, so easily provoked to take to the streets and shout of OCCUPATION – occupy here; occupy there, occupy the south and north poles saturate the air and eventually invade the motherless, homeless child who's been hiding in a secret cave, thus setting off the *"Cry of the Motherless,"* which bemoans a world that is continually engaged in armed conflicts. The motherless thus cries out, *"The only sound I hear in this part is the sound of annihilation – marked by these massive roaming of dead bodies that defied these invasive swarming of countless hungry Vultures. ...And like my implosion, the world's been turned into a molecular time bomb".*

What makes the inhabitants of the earth brew with so much hate and antagonism? Could this be the case of *"Cain and Abel?"* But there's another culture that should worry you: a culture of culpability of the United Nations (the UN and its organs) in preserving the earth, preventing wars, and Uniting the Nations. Religious ideologies and extremism are another playbook deployed by these instruments of destabilization to push the universe towards precipice, making millions of people shudder at *"This Kind of Color"*. The bulldog posturing of the UN Security Council, political and religious extremism and the audacity of tyrannical leaders are nudging the doomsday clock to the doomsday hour. But authoritarians are swiftly warned to beware of *"The Way of All Tyrants"*, whose *"end shall come like a gloaming upon a city"*. A peep into these situations finds *"Mama Africa, still groping in Darkness,* subsumed in "Forced and Unforced" errors – a place of illusion orchestrated and imposed on her by *"Merchants of Wars"* and *"Our Slave Masters"* who turn the continent into scenes of bloodletting while inciting brothers and sisters, kits and kins into wars, killings, maiming and wanton destruction of their own lives and homes. Africa is yet to realize that *"Life is a Discovery."* Thus, the Africa of this age must ask new questions and seek and pursue new answers to champion its own course. And after about 25 years of uninterrupted civilian governance in Nigeria, the country remains a far cry from what it was in the 1970s and early 80s. Somehow the masses now cry out, *"Bring Back those Days!"*. Though, this is not the only sound coming out of Nigeria. There is the *"Cry of the Childless"* woman, personified by the albatross and the conundrum of oil exploration in the Niger Delta region of the country.

But when you look more closely at the world, you will see only two predominantly classes of people: *"The Nobles and the Miserables"* – plus *"The Dancing Sun"* – a mysterious event that happens around the world. The author poetically dramatizes this phenomenon in a graphical illustration of one of the incidents.

The Book features free verse, classical poetry, rhymes, sonnets, and dramatized epic narratives. Be careful when you handle *"The Dancing Sun"*. It can make you smile, cry, or even laugh.